TIMES PAST
BUT
NOT FORGOTTEN
A Walk By Faith Down Memory Lane

JOHN MARINELLI

Times Past But Not Forgotten: A Walk by Faith Down Memory Lane
Copyright © 2021 by Rev. John Marinelli
All rights reserved.
Second Edition: 2026

Contact:
P. O. Box 831413
Ocala, FL. 34483
johnmarinelli@embarqmail.com

Cover and Formatting: Streetlight Graphics

Print ISBN: 978-1087950563
eBook ISBN: 978-1087950570

This book is protected by the United States Copyright Laws. Any use whatsoever is prohibited without written permission from the author.

No part of this book may be reproduced, scanned, or distributed in any printed or electronic form without permission. Please do not participate in or encourage piracy of copyrighted materials in violation of the author's rights. Thank you for respecting the hard work of this author.

TABLE OF CONTENTS

Preface v

Introduction vii

Chapter One
    Stinking Thinking 1

Chapter Two
    My Brain Hemorrhage 5

Chapter Three
    The Birth of A New Me 10

Chapter Four
    Two Natures In Conflict 15

Chapter Five
    The Intersection 20

Chapter Six
    Scarlet Fever 24

Chapter Seven
    My, "One Way," Dilemma 26

Chapter Eight

My Encounter With Jesus …… 36

Chapter Nine
My Cheerleader …… 39

Chapter Ten
Walking Through The Titles …… 41

Chapter Eleven
Free At Last …… 47

Chapter Twelve
Living In The Spirit …… 55

Chapter Thirteen
The Great Epiphany …… 63

Chapter Fourteen
For Love or Money …… 68

Chapter Fifteen
Ketoacidosis Comma …… 73

Chapter Sixteen
The Covid-19 Attack …… 76

Chapter Seventeen
The Anointing …… 78

Conclusion …… 81
About The Author …… 83

PREFACE

"Times Past But Not Forgotten" is a walk by faith down memory lane. It is a look back into the life of the author to examine the effects of Biblical faith on his life and those close to him. The author will present the events in the order he remembers them, not chronologically.

The author's goal in writing this book is to present a teaching on faith and what it can accomplish in the life of a believer.

This is a true story. The events described are real. They actually happened. Some will be perceived as small and insignificant, while others as dynamic, even bordering on miraculous.

Other folks will be included in the discussions as they relate to the application of faith and the Christian lifestyle.

INTRODUCTION

Do you believe in time travel? How wonderful it would be to go back in time and right all the wrongs and change all the events so we would come out of the experiences free of guilt, sorrow, or any other form of suffering.

Life has a way of beating us up and leaving us to die, without hope or emotional stability. We grow old, and then what? Our future is dim, and our memories fade away, and then we die...unless we take dominion and continue to live.

Most of the senior folks that I know major on the minors in life. That is to say, they dwell on that which does not exist anymore.

Yes, the hurts were real and the suffering enormous, but they all qualify as *"Times Past But Not Forgotten."* We hang on to them and rehearse them in our minds, re-living them repeatedly. Sometimes it is by choice and other times involuntary through flashbacks from trauma.

As we look back, we will look at the victories, not the defeats. We will try to learn from each encounter, establishing a secure foundation.

CHAPTER ONE

Stinking Thinking

How about I give you a penny for your thoughts? I would like to know what you are thinking about. After all, I am not a mind reader.

Tell me what you are thinking so I can criticize you for being negative and rude. Isn't that what is going on inside your head?

Some folks live in a world of negativity that could easily be construed as, "Stinking Thinking"

I used to be one of those folks. I had a negative outlook on life and saw everything through an egotistical filter. That was a long time ago. I did not realize that life could be rewarding and that I could be positive in my expectations of it.

The Bible tells us to stop thinking of the negative and otherwise sad things and to dwell on the positive aspects of life. Here is what the apostle Paul said to the first - century church:

> *Finally, brethren, whatsoever things are true, whatsoever things are honest, whatsoever things*

> *are just, whatsoever things are pure, whatsoever things are lovely, whatsoever things are of good report; if there be any virtue, and if there be any praise, think on these things."* Philippians 4:8

Paul also instructs the early believers on lifestyle. He says;

> *" Be careful for nothing; but in every thing by prayer and supplication with thanksgiving let your requests be made known unto God.*
>
> *And the peace of God, which passes all understanding, shall keep your hearts and minds through Christ Jesus."* Philippians 4:6-8

Paul apparently knew that dwelling on good things would keep our hearts vibrant and alive so we could actually experience the abundant life that Jesus spoke of in John 10:10. Read it for yourself:

> *"The thief comes not, but for to steal, and to kill, and to destroy: I am come that they might have life, and that they might have it more abundantly."*

Paul was a man who lived out what he preached. He was nothing like the leaders of today, who follow a "Do As I Say & Not As I Do" philosophy. Listen to what he said about his past;

> *"Brethren, I count not myself to have apprehended: but this one thing I do, forgetting those things which are behind, and reaching forth unto those things which are before, I press toward the mark for the*

prize of the high calling of God in Christ Jesus."
Philippians 3:13-14

Notice where his eyes are. They are not in the past but the future, and he is pressing on towards his destiny in Christ. Don't you think we should do the same?

My perspective was off. I used to be a positive sort of guy, but because of circumstances beyond my control, I succumbed to an angry spirit, and it changed the way I looked at life.

There was no point in trying anymore because life will disappoint you, and you will be left in the cold.

All this negativity played out in my life when I was a young man, before I saw the truths of the Bible and received its godly counsel.

However, once enlightened, I thought on these things, things that were pure, happy and of good report. Let me tell you that the transformation from negative to positive was really hard. It took all the faith I had and then some. My natural inclination was to be critical of people and situations.

I kept telling myself that I would not criticize. Many times I told myself to shut up. My self-talk became one big argument. I found myself arguing with myself.

Eventually, my desire to be positive won out. I had won the argument. From that point on, I began rejecting anything negative and actively searched for good things to think about.

I figured it this way…if Paul said we should think of good things, then it was possible for me to do so…and I did.

CHAPTER TWO

My Brain Hemorrhage

It was March 29th 1945, the day of my birth. I survived the trauma of birth, only to end up in critical condition with a brain hemorrhage. Doctors did not expect me to live. Had it not been for the prayers of my relatives and family, I would not be here today.

I started out as a healthy 8 lb. baby boy, but by the time I was 6-weeks old, I suffered a massive brain hemorrhage.

Candles were lit in the Catholic church. My mother prayed and dedicated my life to God if He would allow me to live. Many other relatives prayed and sought the Lord for my life.

What is it about prayer that changes things? I should have passed away, yet I am here and have already celebrated my 80th birthday. It is all because of the prayers of others.

When we pray, we acknowledge our frailty and need for God's help. However, prayer without belief is useless. Believing is another word for faith. Here is what the Bible says about faith;

" *But without faith it is impossible to please him: for he that comes to God must believe that he is, and that he is a rewarder of them that diligently seek him."* Hebrews 11:6

The scripture tells us that when we come to God in prayer; we believe God does really exist and that He rewards those who actually believe in Him.

We also know from this scripture that without faith, it is impossible to please God.

So, what is Faith? We need to know. We will need it to please God and get our prayers answered. Again, we'll turn to the scriptures:

"Now faith is the substance of things hoped for, the evidence of things not seen." Hebrews 11:1.

First of all, when you believe, you have faith. That is what it is. It is the act of believing. When you believe, you demonstrate faith.

Second, you will create your desired outcome by believing.

Finally, your belief/faith is the evidence or proof that what you asked for will come to be.

In other words, your believing is making what does not exist…(*not yet seen*). It will materialize if you continue to believe.

It is not difficult to understand. Let us say you ask God for a husband or wife. You meet all the qualifiers, which are:

1. **You are asking in accordance to His Will.**

    "Ye ask, and receive not, because ye ask amiss, that ye may consume it upon your lusts." James 4:3

2. **You are confident that God is listening and attentive to your needs.**

"And this is the confidence that we have in him, that, if we ask any thing according to his will, he hears us and if we know that he hear us, whatsoever we ask, we know that we have the petitions that we desired of him." I John 5:14-15

3. **You are actively striving to keep His commandments.**

"And whatsoever we ask, we receive of him, because we keep his commandments, and do those things that are pleasing in his sight." I John 3:22

However, which commandments do you keep? Which ones are pleasing in His sight? All the commandments revolve around loving God and our neighbor. Hear what Jesus said:

"Master, which is the great commandment in the law? Jesus said unto him, Thou shalt love the Lord thy God with all thy heart, and with all thy soul, and with all thy mind. This is the first and great commandment. And the second is like unto it, Thou shalt love thy neighbor as thyself. On these two commandments hang all the law and the prophets." Matthew 22:36-40

4. **You believe God will give you what you ask for, as you trust in Him.**

"And all things, whatsoever ye shall ask in prayer, believing, ye shall receive." Matthew 21:22

5. **You delight yourself in the Lord and enjoy being in His presence.**

"Delight thyself also in the LORD; and he shall give thee the desires of thine heart." Psalm 37:4

6. **You are chosen of God and ready to do His will.**

"Ye have not chosen me, but I have chosen you, and ordained you, that ye should go and bring forth fruit, and [that] your fruit should remain: that whatsoever ye shall ask of the Father in my name, he may give it you." John 15:16

7. **You are hiding the Word of God in your heart and applying its truth to your life situations.**

"If ye abide in me, and my words abide in you, ye shall ask what ye will, and it shall be done unto you." John15:7.

So, doesn't it make sense that God will give you your request? All you have to do is believe. The rest of the qualifiers that I mentioned above are part of your Christian walk with the Lord.

These are the things that make our faith live. This is the

evidence that what has not as yet been seen will in fact arrive in God's timing.

My childhood brain hemorrhage was healed. The prayers of my family became the substance from which my restoration was derived. If that is not a miracle, I do not know what is.

CHAPTER THREE

The Birth of A New Me

I was left to fend for myself as I grew up. My parents worked hard and were not around when school was out. On weekends, I ran around with kids of all sorts, some good and some not. Habits formed like smoking cigarettes made from old butts found along the side of the road or a corn- cob pipe with pine needles as tobacco.

I was on a path that led to destruction and was full of mischief and rebellion. However, my mother was a Southern Baptist who was a member of a small church that once a year had a week of intense Bible activities for kids. They called it "Vacation Bible School."

Needless to say, I ended up there. I was immediately involved in Bible stories and discussions about the salvation of the soul.

I was counseled and shown in the Bible why it was so important to be, "Born Again." I had already lived 8-years and did not see any need to get born again. However, I realized that my lifestyle, even as a young adult, was not pleasing to God.

Here is what I saw in the scriptures as I read the 3rd chapter of John. Listen to the story as recorded by John, the Apostle.

> *"There was a man of the Pharisees named Nicodemus, a ruler of the Jews. This man came to Jesus by night and said to Him, "Rabbi, we know that You are a teacher come from God; for no one can do these signs that You do unless God is with him."*
>
> *Jesus answered and said to him, "Most assuredly, I say to you, unless one is born again, he cannot see the kingdom of God."*
>
> *Nicodemus said to Him, "How can a man be born when he is old? Can he enter a second time into his mother's womb and be born?"*
>
> *Jesus answered, "Most assuredly, I say to you, unless one is born of water and the Spirit, he cannot enter the kingdom of God. That which is born of the flesh is flesh, and that which is born of the Spirit is spirit.*
>
> *Do not marvel that I said to you, 'You must be born again.' The wind blows where it wishes, and you hear the sound of it, but cannot tell where it comes from and where it goes. So is everyone who is born of the Spirit."*

Nicodemus answered and said to Him, "How can these things be?"

Jesus answered and said to him, "Are you the teacher of Israel, and do not know these things? Most assuredly, I say to you, We speak what We know and testify what We have seen, and you do not receive Our witness.

If I have told you earthly things and you do not believe, how will you believe if I tell you heavenly things? No one has ascended to heaven but He who came down from heaven, that is, the Son of Man who is in heaven. And as Moses lifted up the serpent in the wilderness, even so must the Son of Man be lifted up, that whoever believes in Him should not perish but have eternal life.

For God so loved the world that He gave His only begotten Son, that whoever believes in Him should not perish but have everlasting life. For God did not send His Son into the world to condemn the world, but that the world through Him might be saved. **John 3:1-17.**

Nicodemus was a ruler of the Jews. That would be equivalent to being a pastor or Bible teacher today. He was a member of an established religious group. He was a man of authority, wisdom and one who was educated in the things of God. However, like many religious leaders of our day, he lacked the simple truth that makes a person a child of God.

It is not religion, being nice, doing good works, being smart, and wealthy or any earthly thing. Jesus qualified it by saying you need a second birth, that of the Spirit, to see and enter His kingdom.

This can only happen by believing in Jesus, who is the only begotten Son of God. The first birth is not eternal because of sin, but the second is eternal because of Christ. (See Romans Chapter 5)

The question is, are all the peoples of the earth children of God? I think it is important to examine why Jesus said, *"You Must Be "Born Again"* He was talking to Nicodemus, a ruler of the Jews of that day.

Jesus told him that even his extensive study and dedication to religion would not get him into the kingdom of God. It would take a new birth experience.

I saw myself walking through life devoid of spiritual insight. That was quite a revelation for a 8-year-old kid. The Holy Spirit led me to a place where I could see my sin and how it was offensive to God. He also made me realize I was cut off from God and doomed to an eternal hell in my current state. I was tried, convicted, and sentenced to death all in one day. However, the same Spirit of God led me to John 3:16 and showed me how I could beat the rap and go free.

I could become a, "whosoever" and believe in Jesus, and

He would give me a new heart and life that would please God, the Father. I could become a child of God.

The Vacation Bible School leaders made sure I understood the significance of my decision to be "Born Again." I would have to repent and ask for God's forgiveness. Then, I would have to change my direction from doing evil to doing the will of God.

I took it seriously and committed myself to following Jesus. I began to read the Bible and associate with other like-minded folks. I grew in my knowledge, but even more fantastic was the fact that I was actually walking <u>in the Spirit</u>.

I was hearing the voice of God and learning what His will is for my life. He was confirming my acceptance as a child of God. We had a relationship in the Spirit and it was full of love and blessings. It was great. It still is.

CHAPTER FOUR

Two Natures In Conflict

Before I was" Born Again," I operated in just one nature, and that nature was sinful and self-absorbed. The deeds of that lifestyle manifested as jealously, pride, selfishness, disobedience, lust, and a lot of unpleasant personality traits. I cared for myself and no one else unless it was to advance my agenda.

After I became" Born Again," I saw a new nature forming inside of me. This was really interesting because I found myself slowly changing.

The unpleasant personality traits gave way to Godly attributes like joy, love, peace, longsuffering, gentleness, etc. (Galatians Chapter five)

However, my before nature and after nature fought each other for control of my thoughts and actions. My mind became a battlefield. The Spirit and the Flesh were in a life-or-death struggle for me.

Suddenly I saw how the sinful nature manifested itself and how the new man battled to destroy the works of the Flesh. It was like I was watching a movie. But I played the leading role in the story. I felt terrible as I kept seeing my true self, full of evil and egotistical thoughts. But then I read in the scriptures where the apostle Paul struggled with the same problem.

> *"For the good that I would, I do not: but the evil which I would not, that I do. Now if I do that I would not, it is no more I that do it, but sin that dwells in me. I find then a law, that, when I would do good, evil is present with me. For I delight in the law of God after the inward man."*
>
> *"But I see another law in my members, warring against the law of my mind, and bringing me into captivity to the law of sin, which is in my members."*
>
> *"O wretched man that I am! Who shall deliver me from the body of this death? I thank God through Jesus Christ our Lord."*
>
> *"So then with the mind I myself serve the law of God; but with the flesh the law of sin."* Romans 7:19-25

This is a great word picture of what is going on inside of every "Born Again" Christian. It is two natures in conflict, and Paul separates himself from the battle and thanks God for deliverance.

He saw the evil at work in himself and cried out to God for help. He hoped to live godly in Christ Jesus without dragging around his old nature of sin.

Paul is our example. We can also conclude that the sinful nature in us is no longer us. We are dead to sin and alive to righteousness. This attitude, of course, is an act of faith. We believe we are new creatures and therefore free to serve the Lord. Here is the proof text to this assertion.

> *"Therefore if any man be in Christ, he is a new creature: old things are passed away; behold, all things are become new."* 2 Corinthians 5:17

The new creature is that new nature that formed in us when we were "Born Again."

I see the butterfly as an impressive picture of the new creature in Christ.

All Things Become NEW

BE A BUTTERFLY

Be A Butterfly
And fly away with me.
We'll fly with God's Promises
Straight into eternity.

Be a butterfly
To crawl no more
But to soar in the Spirit
Above evil's mighty roar.

Be a butterfly
To fly to heights unknown,
Soaring on the wings of faith,
Never more to be alone.

Be a butterfly
And fly away with me,
For God has made us new.
At last! At Last! We are free.

By John Marinelli
9/23/86

Paul also tells us he has been crucified with Christ, but he still lives. Here is what he said.

> *"I am crucified with Christ: nevertheless I live; yet not I, but Christ lives in me: and the life which I now live in the flesh I live by the faith of the Son of God, who loved me, and gave himself for me."*
> Galatians 2:20.

How can that be? He says that his crucifixion with Jesus was to put to death the old man or nature of sin so the life of Christ could flourish within his personality.

He also says that this new life with Jesus would be accomplished by tapping into the faith of the Son of God. He did not have to muster up courage to have faith. The Holy Spirit freely gave it to him so he could live by it.

This process is also at work in us, who believe. We are crucified with Christ and now are new creatures, like the butterfly. We used to be a creepy crawler, but that guy died in the cocoon. What came forth was a butterfly, a totally new creature. This is our destiny.

So, come and be a Butterfly with me.

CHAPTER FIVE

The Intersection

I remember the miracle at the intersection. I was somewhere around 28 years old. I was driving down the road in Orlando, Florida, where I lived. My first wife was with me. She was pregnant with my first of two children. His name is Daniel. He is 56 years old as I remember this event. But then he was not yet born.

The stoplight turned from green to amber. I was in a hurry going nowhere fast and sped up to beat the caution light before it turned red.

As I sped up, another vehicle turned right in front of me. There was no way I could have missed hitting it. I hit my brakes, but they just locked up. I was burning rubber and sliding through the intersection. I should have hit the other vehicle broadside, but somehow, I did not.

I swear it felt like I had entered a slow-motion zone. Everything slowed down except the other vehicle. It was still moving at regular speed. I could do nothing but sit still and watch the other guy pass in front of me. It seemed like a long time but was only seconds.

When the other vehicle was clear of my car, I began to speed up and continued to slide through the intersection. It was a strange feeling.

I knew God had sent His angel to protect me and ensure the normal birth of my son. It was a true miracle.

I did not have time to cry out to God, even though I mumbled, "Oh dear God." I was still relying on the scriptures to keep me, even though I made a mistake in trying to beat the light at the intersection.

I believe God has given us precious promises in the Bible that, if held dear to our hearts, will guide our lives and keep us out of harm's way.

A few years ago, the Lord showed me that these precious promises were actually spiritual hooks. When we read them, we can place our faith on one or more of the hooks, and it will remain there as long as we continue to believe.

Here is the hook I hung my faith on many years ago and still believe.

> *"The angel of the Lord encamps round about them that fear him, and delivers them."* Psalm 34:7.

The word "Fear" is better translated as "Reverence." Deliverance comes through reverence and respect for God and a belief that He will be there with His angels to help you in times of trouble. That is exactly what happened. It was a miracle for sure.

Did you know that there are over 3,000 promises in the Bible? That means there are over 3,000 spiritual hooks available to us. We can hook our faith on one, some or all if we want.

Check it out sometime. Read the Bible until you see a promise. The Holy Spirit will open the eyes of your understanding so you can see which hook to put your faith on.

I know there are some that might read this and say, "I do not have enough faith to believe like this guy says. The truth is, you do not need much. Hear what Jesus said about faith.

> *"For verily I say unto you, If ye have faith as a grain of mustard seed, ye shall say unto this mountain, Remove hence to yonder place; and it shall remove; and nothing shall be impossible unto you."* Matthew 17:20.

A mustard seed is probably the smallest seed there is, yet it holds the power to move mountains when exercised by a person of faith.

THE ANGEL'S CAMP

The Angel of the Lord
Sets up his camp
Around those who reverence God.

Imagine being there
In the midst of
Where angels trod.

What a joy it is
To know God's protection
And to be in the angel's camp.

It is there that God's children
Are delivered from evil's woe,
And led by the Word, heaven's lamp.

Poem By: John Marinelli

"The angel of the Lord encamps round about them that fear Him, and delivers them" Psalm 34:7

CHAPTER SIX

Scarlet Fever

My son, Daniel, was about one-year-old when he came down with scarlet fever. I thought it had been wiped off the face of the earth in the late 1800s and early 1900s. None-the-less, he had it, and it was terrible.

Scarlet fever is an infectious bacterial disease affecting especially children, and causing fever and a scarlet rash. It was worse between 1820 and 1880. There was a worldwide pandemic of scarlet fever, and several severe epidemics occurred in Europe and North America.

I went to church that Sunday morning with a heavy heart. All the medication and care had not worked. My son was getting worse.

At the end of the service, the pastor called for prayer requests and for people to speak them before the congregation. So, I did just that. With a trembling voice, I almost yelled my request. "Please pray for my son. He has scarlet fever and is not getting better."

The entire church prayed, and the pastor came against the fever and commanded it to go…in the name of Jesus. It was a serious prayer by all the folks in the church, about 200.

When I arrived home from church, my son had been healed. The fever broke at the same time we were praying. It was a miracle.

My son grew up healthy and became an aircraft mechanic for Learjets. He is now a supervisor.

The faith of God's children healed my son, and the power of corporate prayer was demonstrated that Sunday. The doctors were not effective. It took prayer and faith that God would move on my behalf.

The scripture that I held on to and hooked my faith on… well, see it for yourself and you decide.

> *"Again I say unto you, That if two of you shall agree on earth as touching any thing that they shall ask, it shall be done for them of my Father which is in heaven. For where two or three are gathered together in my name, there am I in the midst of them.."* Matthew 18:19-20

Over 200 believers came to God in prayer, believing that He would answer their request for healing. Now that is a miracle.

CHAPTER SEVEN

My "One Way" Dilemma

Have you ever been driving on a street that only goes one way? A one-way street only goes one way. Imagine that? That is why they call it a one-way street.

What happens when that one-way is the only way to reach a destination? Contrary to popular belief, all roads did not lead to Rome. Some went to other destinations.

I want you to think about going to heaven. Do all religions lead there? Or is there only one-way?

When I was a new believer, I discovered that Jesus was and still is the only way to heaven. I had some problems with that doctrine at first because it left out all other religions. They were considered to be false teachings.

My "Born Again" experience brought with it the Biblical truth that Jesus is the only way to God, the Father. However, I could not accept that premise without further research, so I turned to the Bible for a look-see.

The Bible is our source for proving that the one-way doctrine is valid. **Acts 4:12** says,

> *"Neither is there salvation in any other: for there is*

none other name under heaven given among men, whereby we must be saved."

Here is why it is so important. Adam sinned against God and died spiritually.

> *"And the Lord God commanded the man, saying, Of every tree of the garden thou may freely eat: But of the tree of the knowledge of good and evil, thou shalt not eat of it: for in the day that thou eat thereof thou shalt surely die."* **Genesis 2:16-17.**

The creation account shows Adam being made of clay and God breathing into him the "Breath of Life." He thus became a living soul.

> *"And the Lord God formed man of the dust of the ground, and breathed into his nostrils the breath of life; and man became a living soul."* **Genesis 2:7.**

When he sinned, this, "Breath of Life," was taken from him, and he became a dead soul. He was truly the first of the walking dead.

Life is always in relationship to God. It is His breath or Spirit that makes us alive.

> *"So, death passed upon all men for all sinned."* **(Romans 5:12).**

Their nature was now sinful. We see this in all of us and in our societies.

The second birth experience is of the Spirit. The "Breath

of Life" is restored or given to each repentant heart, and their souls become alive to God. They become His children through faith in Jesus, God's only begotten Son. Jesus is the only way to attain salvation.

All the world religions cannot save us. Joining a church or a specific faith cannot save us. It must be an acknowledgment of our sin, our cry before the throne of God for forgiveness, and our invitation to Jesus to come into our hearts and save us. His name is the only name that can get us through death into eternal life.

Here are a few scriptures that support the only "One-Way" doctrine.

1. *...there is one God, and one mediator between God and men, the man Christ Jesus; Who gave himself a ransom for all, to be testified in due time.* **(I Timothy 2:5-6)**

2. *...Believe on the Lord Jesus Christ and thou shalt be saved...* **(Acts 16:31)**

3. *That if thou shalt confess with thy mouth the Lord Jesus, and shalt believe in thine heart that God hath raised him from the dead, THOU SHALT BE SAVED. For with the heart man believeth unto righteousness; and with the mouth confession is made unto salvation.* **(Romans 10:9-10)**

The skeptic would say," You mean to tell me that all the religions of the world are wrong and only Christianity is the one true religion?"

No, that is not what I am saying. Remember, Christianity is not a religion. It is a relationship born out of love between man and the one true and living God. There is no one true religion. Religion in itself will not get us to God.

It is the blood of Christ that unlocks the door, and our confession of faith in Jesus that makes it all happen. **(John 14:6)**

Why is Jesus the only way to God? Because God planned it that way. He set the penalty for sin, which was death.

> *"The soul that sinneth, it shall die."* **(Ezekiel 18:20)**

In fact, Jesus was the slain Lamb of God before the foundation of the world. **(Ephesians 1:3-7)**

Jesus Himself said, as recorded in John 14:6,

> *"I am the way, the truth, and the life: no man comes to the Father but by Me."*

Christianity states that the God of the Bible is the only true God, and that salvation is only possible by accepting Jesus Christ, His only begotten Son, as Savior and Lord.

II Corinthians 5:21 says,

> *"For he hath made him to be sin for us, who knew no sin; that we might be made the righteousness of God in him."*

Validation

God validated His Son as the only way in multiple ways so we could be assured that Jesus was indeed the only way to Him. Here are some to consider.

1. He claimed to be the only way, as in John's record 14:6 says, but validation came through miracles that proved He was who He claimed to be.
2. Eyewitnesses saw Jesus' miracles and validated them as authentic. Over 500 followers saw Jesus after His resurrection and watched Him ascend into heaven.
3. The prophets foretold of His coming, where He would be born, that He would be God in human flesh and lots more…all prophetic statements were realized in Jesus, even those like in Isaiah chapter 53 that were uttered hundreds of years before Jesus came.
4. God Himself validated Jesus as His sole pathway to Him.

"While he was still speaking, behold, a bright cloud overshadowed them; and suddenly a voice came out of the cloud, saying, "This is My beloved Son, in whom I am well pleased. Hear ye Him!" **(Matthew 17:5)**

5. The apostles lost their homes, wealth, and even

their lives preaching the gospel. Would they do that if it were a lie? I do not think so. They testified to the truth and were willing to die for it if necessary. (Read Foxes Book of Martyrs)

6. Thousands of Believers, over several centuries have testified of how Jesus helped them and blessed them.
7. I can personally testify that I have seen the hand of the Lord in my life and communicate with Him daily. I know He is the Christ.

The probability that one man could fulfill all prophecies about a Messiah that God Himself said would come, **(Gen.3:15)**, and perform fantastic miracles while here on earth, and be raised from the dead, and ascend into heaven while hundreds looked on is astronomical.

But Jesus did just that…fulfilled everything that was foretold about the coming Messiah. He had to be who He said He was and therefore is truly the only way to God.

It should be obvious by now that it is essential for anyone who wants eternal life to be "Born Again." **Romans 10:9-10** will tell us how.

> *"That if thou shalt confess with thy mouth the Lord Jesus, and shalt believe in thine heart that God hath raised him from the dead, thou shalt be saved.* [10] *For with the heart man believeth unto righteousness; and with the mouth confession is made unto salvation."* **Romans 10:9-10.**

Confessing Jesus is to acknowledge His Lordship and openly proclaim your allegiance. There is no secret society. That is why the scripture says, *"With Thy Mouth."*

Believing with the heart is different from believing with the mind. When we believe with our heart, it means relying upon, adhering to and trusting in. We are to wholly embrace the truth that God raised up Jesus from the dead after being crucified for the sins of mankind.

Remember what Paul wrote to the Romans in Chapter 5. He said that Adam was the 1st man who fell into sin and took the entire race with him. Thus, death passed upon all of us.

However, Jesus was the second Adam or last man that was sent outside of the pollution of human sinful DNA via a virgin birth to be the spotless Lamb of God and to be slain as a sacrifice for sin to abolish it forever.

Therefore the "New Birth" is necessary to free us from the sin of the 1st Adam and propel us by spiritual birth into the Kingdom of God.

My doubts are all done now. After seeing the truth in the Word of God, I rest easy, knowing that I am a child of God. Plus, I have the Spirit of God confirming my acceptance into the Kingdom of God every hour of every day. This is a miracle.

> *"The Spirit itself bears witness with our spirit, that we are the children of God: And if children, then heirs; heirs of God, and joint-heirs with Christ; if*

so be that we suffer with him, that we may be also glorified together." **Romans 8:15-17.**

We who have believed can say that we are His children, without a doubt or any question in our minds. We can because the Spirit of God is continually bearing witness with our spirits. He leads us; He communicates with us; He teaches us and shows us truth and error. That is how we know for sure.

If you have never seen the hand of God in your life or heard the spirit speaking to you, you might want to go back to God and repent of your sins, ask his forgiveness, and ask Jesus to come into your heart and save you. Then, receive Jesus as your Lord and Savior. This is the only way you can be born again.

Ephesians 2:1-22 ASV says

"And you were dead in your trespasses and sins, in which you formerly walked according to the course of this world, according to the prince of the power of the air, of the spirit that is now working in the sons of disobedience. Among them we too all formerly lived in the lusts of our flesh, indulging the desires of the flesh and of the mind, and were by nature children of wrath, even as the rest.

But God, being rich in mercy, because of His great love with which He loved us, even when we were dead in our transgressions, made us alive together with Christ (by grace you have been saved), and raised us up with Him, and seated us with Him in the heavenly places in Christ Jesus, so that in the ages to come He might show the surpassing riches of His grace in kindness toward us in Christ Jesus.

For by grace you have been saved through faith; and that not of yourselves, it is the gift of God; not as a result of works, so that no one may boast. For we are His workmanship, created in Christ Jesus for good works, which God prepared beforehand so that we would walk in them.

Read this again. It tells you where you were or are now and where God takes you when you are born again. It is truly a life-changing experience. **Ephesians Chapter 2.**

The above scripture passage reveals 10 benefits that overtake the believer at his new birth. They are:

1. We experience God's great mercy and love… verse #4
2. We are made alive to God, given eternal life… verse #5
3. We were raised up with Christ and seated with Him in heavenly places…. verse #6
4. We receive His Grace or unmerited favor… Verse # 8
5. We are brought close to God through the blood of Christ…verse #13
6. Jesus becomes our peace…verse #14

7. We gain access to God through His Spirit… verse #18
8. We are no longer strangers but fellow citizens and joint heirs with Christ…verse 19
9. We are becoming a spiritual dwelling for God…verse #22
10. We are His workmanship, created in Christ Jesus unto good works that were established before we were saved so we could walk in them…v#10
11. We have discussed how Jesus really is the only pathway to God, the Father. We have looked at benefits of being, "Born Again," and why it is necessary to attain eternal life.

We have seen how to be "Born Again" through repentance, a plea for forgiveness and an invitation to Jesus to enter our hearts and be our Savior and Lord.

There is only one thing left to do: decide if you are "Born Again" or not. If not, go before the Lord and ask to be born into His kingdom. Then follow His teachings.

The butterfly is a great example of a sinner being transformed into a child of God. It is a true miracle. Let it be the picture of your new birth.

CHAPTER EIGHT

My Encounter With Jesus

Between 1979 and 1982, I was the Executive Director of the Davie/Cooper City Chamber of Commerce located in Davie, Florida. I was recently divorced and backslidden from the things of God.

I was a chaser of skirts and had become the, "Fair Haired" boy of the local business world. I was going places fast and loved by most everyone. They loved my dedication and hard work. They loved my lecherous personality. They looked up to me as a somebody.

Several years before, I was a Bible student preparing to be a minister of the gospel. Me and God were as tight as we could be. But my divorce stripped me of my faith and hurled me into a world of confusion.

I was lost and undone, falling back into the world system of things. The things of God were replaced with the things of this world system.

It was a very stressful time. I could be spiritual as long as I kept it in line with the apostate church of Universalism.

I had to give up Jesus to embrace the world. What Jesus said was true.

"No man can serve two masters: for either he will hate the one, and love the other; or else he will hold to the one, and despise the other. Ye cannot serve God and mammon.(Money)" Matthew 6:24.

As I fell backwards into my past sinful lifestyle, I still cried unto the Lord for help. It was apparent even to me that I was out of control.

Now here is the best part of my story. My now second wife came into my office seeking employment. Long story short, she was hired and eventually became my office manager. She was a new Christian, single and beautiful.

She could see right through me. She would pester me with questions about the Bible and why I was so mad at God.

One day during a pestering session, when she was asking questions, I saw Jesus. He entered my office and began talking to me. I saw Him in the Spirit, not the flesh. I could feel His presence and hear His voice above all other voices.

He said just one thing: *"It is a long way back. Are you ready to walk with me again?"*

I cried out to Him in my spirit, saying, "Yes, Lord," I am ready. That was more than 40 years ago. I am still walking with Jesus. He delivered me and led me back to a victorious Christian life.

I married my office manager and am about to celebrate

my 44th wedding anniversary. It has been a trip, an uphill battle through lots of difficult times, but I am still here, by the grace of God. It is a miracle.

CHAPTER NINE

My Cheerleader

Have you ever been down and out, sad, and blue, feeling bad all the time? I have and it is not a good place to be. I can remember calling out to God and saying, "Why Me Lord?"

It was 1981 when I was running the Chamber of Commerce. I had been divorced for two years after 10 years of marriage and two kids. My mental state was not very good.

I can remember asking Jesus to send me a nice Christian woman who would help me find my way back to Him.

He answered my prayer, but not in the way I expected. Instead of a quiet Christian lady, I got a Bronx New Yorker, outspoken, full of life, energy and fight.

She quickly learned that I was angry with God and called me out on it saying, "Why are you so mad at God?"

This New York babe was a real pain in the butt. However, the more she challenged me, the more I liked her. She was a real cheerleader, always doing the razzle-dazzle to get me motivated.

I likened her to my first crush in high school. She was a cheerleader, about the same height and figure as my wife. I missed the first cheerleader but redeemed the time through my Bronx Babe. She single-handedly, under the anointing of the Holy Spirit, brought me back to the Lord.

I can remember telling God that I had no idea how I could ever again be close to Him. I just did not have it in me. However, I did not need to know how. God knew how, and He was there for me.

It is a great feeling to know the Lord accepts you and you are under His blessings and protection. It was truly a miracle.

CHAPTER TEN

Walking Through The Titles

Most people define their existence through a title. They are a cop, a teacher, a housewife, a truck driver, a scientist, or some other titled walk in life. The title defines them and sets their station in life.

I can remember years ago when I resigned as the Executive Director of a Chamber of Commerce. It was a difficult time, a time when I was just coming back to the Lord after several years of sliding back into the world system and sin.

My wife asked me a simple question: **"Who are you?"** At that time in my life, I could not tell her, because I did not know.

I had, like most of us, fallen into a subtle snare of the devil that led me to define my life and existence by titles. If I were no longer the Executive Director, then…who was I?

My wife kept asking me to tell her who I was. You see, she really needed to know, so she could stand next to me in love and marriage…. But I did not know…because I had lost myself in the maze of titles and expectations of others.

My problem was in how I defined myself. As a Christian, I now know that I am to define myself in relationship, not in titles. Once I saw the truth, it set me free.

The title is just a job. But the relationship lives on, growing with every encounter. It is safe from downsizing, economic shortfalls, management changes, and other worldly expectations.

We, as children of the living God, are to define ourselves by the relationship we have with Him. Think about that for a moment. Most of us lose ourselves because we do not have a close walk with Jesus. Without His voice and presence, we are lost, only to wander in the maze of titles.

He even said, "My sheep hear my voice", yet some would criticize, saying that we are off our rocker because we believe we are hearing from God.

When we define our existence by the quality of the relationship we have with Jesus, we realize our true identity and destiny. We discover His love, His mercy, His faithfulness, and His plan for our well-being.

Remember what the scriptures say…that we are to be conformed to His image and likeness. (Romans 8:28-30) Only a relationship with Him can produce that. It is not found in a title or in book learning. It is in our walk with the Lord.

The term "Christian" was first coined in Antioch, where they called the first believers Christian, because they were seen as "little Christs." Their relationship with Jesus produced the same spirit that was in Jesus. Paul explains this to us in Galatians, chapter five, where he discusses the fruit of the Spirit…Love, Peace, Joy, longsuffering, etc.

"If that same Spirit that raised up Christ Jesus from the dead dwells in you, He shall quicken your mortal flesh and make it alive."

We must learn to walk through the titles and allow the Lord to energize us for true ministry.

It does not matter if we are homemakers, teachers, cops or any other profession. What really matters is that we are experiencing a close relationship with the Lord. It is the only way to know that we are loved and accepted. That is what life is all about. We are quickened or made alive to God in this flesh, through Jesus.

What title is holding you captive? How do you define your existence?

If you are made alive in relationship to God, by the quickening of your spirit, your life will reflect it and no title can ever define your purpose for living.

Only God and His never-ending love can ultimately define our existence and shape our destiny. Remember, we are made in His image with the capacity to fellowship with Him and communicate all of what we hear and see as we walk with Him in this life. That's the essence of who we really are.

I live about 30 minutes north of The Villages. It is a very large retirement community that has folks from all over the US living side by side.

All of them are retired. They were once a doctor, lawyer, cop, or some other titled individual. Now they are all has-beens. They can only look back and say, "I use to be." Many have difficulty defining themselves now because they no longer hold a position.

I FIND MYSELF IN GOD

I find myself in God.
He is my "Everything."
I know that He is Lord,
My life, my hope, and King.

I find myself in God,
Not the ways of sin.
Nor do I look to others,
To know who I really am.

I find myself in God,
To whom I bow on bended knee.
He alone is my joy and strength
And where I want to be.

Written By
Rev. John Marinelli

Sometimes, like with me, it takes a miracle to find yourself, but doing so is what makes you happy. It motivates you and keeps you in difficult times.

We Christian folk can only find peace and happiness by

connecting with God and staying close to Jesus. Abiding in the vine (Jesus) and concentrating on spiritual things is the only way to be happy.

CHAPTER ELEVEN

Free At Last

One day, somewhere in the past, I realized I was not really free. I read in the Bible that I should be free from the works of the devil and the expectations of others. I was in bondage to both.

We Americans celebrate the 4th of July, as a national holiday in honor and memory of our independence from the bondage and rule of the king of England.

We rejoice that we are free from the rule of any foreign power. History tells us that the original 13 colonies were being overtaxed in an effort to steal the very heart of the land for the use and pleasure of a foreign king. This clearly illustrates John 10:10.

> *"The thief comes not, but for to steal, and to kill and to destroy: I am come that they might have life and that they might have it more abundantly"*

Our ancestors revolted against the king and fought off his tyranny until they gained victory, which resulted in a life of great abundance for many…more so than the people of any other land.

We as Christians do also realize that tyranny and bondage comes in many forms and by many kings, both in the natural and spiritual realms.

We need to be free in the natural & spiritual realms. In the natural realm, we fight off the oppressors to preserve our freedom, sending our next generation to die, if necessary, that we may live in peace and freedom.

But what do we do in the spiritual realm to get free and stay free? What type of bondage do we face, and by whom?

This was my dilemma. I was stuck in a sort of void, wondering what to do. Then I read II Corinthians 10:4-12. The passage helped me to understand who my enemy really was and what to do about it.

> *"The weapons of our warfare are not carnal, (Earthly like tanks and war planes), but are mighty to the pulling down of strongholds."*

The Biblical writer understood that God's people were at war in a spiritual battle with an unseen enemy that somehow enters the imagination. Their thoughts or suggestions are meant to call up impure desires from within our old nature. They are used to capture and hold our minds in bondage to the forces of evil. We know this enemy is Satan, the devil, and his entire evil hoard.

True freedom is having the ability to decide our own destiny. It is not found in the things we possess. It is, however, discovered in the truth that comes from our heavenly Father. That is why Jesus said;

> *"Ye shall know the truth and the truth shall set you free"*. John 8:32

He, of course, is the, "Truth," as He proclaimed in John 14:6. He came from the Father and died on the cross at a place called Calvary to set us free.

But our liberty is not to be used as an occasion for sin, so says Paul, but rather an opportunity to serve the Lord.

Paul also said; Galatians chapter five that we should

> *"Stand fast in the liberty where-with Christ has made us free and be not entangled again in the yoke of bondage."* Galatians 5:1

He knew that freedom always comes with a price tag. It cost something to keep it active. There is always a price to pay. We paid the price of freedom, in the natural, with the blood of our sons and daughters that died in foreign lands.

In the spiritual, we pay with our own lives, laid down unto the death. This is the ultimate sacrifice for our own freedom.

Now I know you are going to say that I am straying off the biblical path and going against what the Bible says, not really.

A closer look reveals that Christ has indeed set us free… bought us with a price, His own blood. We are indeed free, but free to do what?

This is the moment of truth, where we all stand in the valley of decision making "Free Will," choices in life that keep us free or lead us back into bondage.

Without our "Free Will" choices on a consistent basis, we will fall and fall hard. That is why we are instructed to *"Put on the whole armor of God", "Stand fast in the liberty" "Resist the devil"* because our freedom can be easily taken away if we do nothing.

Let me show you where it says that we pay the ultimate sacrifice…Revelation chapter 12,

> *"And they (that is us) overcame him (that is the devil) with the blood of the Lamb, the word of their testimony and that they laid down their lives unto the death."*

Most pastors call attention only to the first two parts of this scripture, but it is the third, the laying down of one's own life, which seals the victory.

Jesus supports this "self-death" notion when He tells His disciples that they must deny themselves, take up their crosses (referring to their own death) and follow Him. Luke 9:23.

I could not help but wonder why. Why is it so necessary for us to die in order to live?

Romans Chapter five tells us that sin entered the world (human experience) through the transgression of one man, Adam. It also tells us that through one man, Jesus Christ, all shall be made alive.

As I continued to read, I learned Adam was the first man

and Jesus is the last man. The first man fell into sin and, as a result, death passed upon all men, for all have sinned.

Romans chapter three supports this where it says that all have sinned and come short of the glory of God. Also, there is none righteous, no not one. The wages of sin is death. Death passed upon all men. Get the picture? It is all clearly stated in Romans chapter three.

Holiness, which is another word for the glory of God, was replaced in the first man with sin, in fact, the very nature of Satan.

We are bound to the devil by nature…however, the last man, Jesus, did not sin, has no evil or darkness in Him and as the spotless "Lamb of God" paid the price for sin.

He bought us back, giving us life in relationship to God. Through Him and in Him, we move and live and have our being.

Remember the baptismal picture? We are buried with Him (Jesus) and raised with Him (Jesus) to newness of life.

We are asked, by the very fact of having a free will, to make our own choices, to walk in this new life.

Paul again says that if we live in the Spirit, we should also walk in the Spirit. Galatians 5:25 He also says that we should be transformed by the renewing of our minds, that we may prove what is that perfect and acceptable will of God. (Romans Chapter 12)

There is no Switzerland in the spirit realm. We walk either in the flesh or in the Spirit. We cannot stay neutral. One nature must die so the other can live. We must carry our own crosses, letting rebellion die so the nature of God can grow and become supreme.

This is the ultimate sacrifice: to forgive instead of condemn, to love instead of hate, and so on…Galatians chapter five lists the evil fleshly appetites as well as the fruit of the Spirit.

My transformation from death unto life came slowly as I struggled with denial of fleshly things. I am doing better, but it is an uphill struggle for sure.

Here is how I know I am free:

1. I have a good sense of peace in my heart.
2. I am quick to forgive.
3. I am sensitive to the prompting of the Holy Spirit.
4. I am aware of the fruit of God's Spirit in me.
5. I see the gifts being manifested in me as I follow Him.
6. I have hope for the future and am optimistic about life.

Notice that there are no feelings of depression, anger, hate, or malice of any kind. There is no jealousy.

The deeds of the flesh are bound by death, and the new creature lives in harmony with God and at peace with his neighbor.

However, that same new creature is also a warrior who

stands against the evil nature in himself and the evil actions of those around him.

This is not a passive stand. It is an aggressive walk in the Spirit that says to self and all around. *"get out of my way for I am walking with God."* He is determined to stay free, as God originally intended.

Take a moment this 4th of July, the season of celebrating freedom, to reflect on those things that have you bound. Chances are they are things of the flesh, which tells you that you are in need of a "Death To Self" experience.

There is a need to be transformed by the renewing of your mind. How do we do that? By, as Romans 12 says...*present your bodies as a living sacrifice unto God.*

Paul also tells us in II Corinthians 10:4-7 that we are to use the knowledge of God as a weapon to cast down every imagination.

If you are in bondage, it is by choice.

> *"God has not given you the spirit of fear that leads you back into bondage, but of Power and Love and a Sound mind."* 2nd Timothy 1:7

Life abundant is given only to those who pass through death first. They must at all cost, stand up in the power of Jesus' name to keep it.

This takes guts, prayer and a determination to follow Jesus. It is also the true meaning of Lordship, when Jesus becomes LORD over your flesh and leads you to the cross in a transforming death unto life experience. Thus is the reality.

> *"Though you are dead, yet shall you live"* John 11:25

The flesh is characteristic of the nature of evil. It is where Satan wants you to dwell…so you portray his image on this earth instead of God's.

All that Satan needs to do is to plant a thought or fashion an image in your mind that calls up what is already inside of you.

This is the imagination of II Corinthians 10:4-7. Act upon the thought or image, giving it place, and you fall out of the Spirit into the flesh. Reject the imagination and you put to death the old nature and continue to walk in the Spirit. It's that simple or should I say, that hard?

Being really free is a "Free Will" choice and is a conscious action of the will to keep the flesh in a state of death and the Spirit in control.

We cannot blame God when we make bad choices. We can however, repent, ask for His forgiveness and begin again…this time with a new determination to walk in the Spirit.

Freedom Costs All We Have But It is Well Worth The Effort.

CHAPTER TWELVE

Living In The Spirit

The Bible tells us we should walk in the Spirit. If we can somehow figure it out, we will not fulfill the lust of the flesh.

However, when I was a new Christian, I had a lot of questions that caused me to stumble as I tried to find God in my everyday life. Here are a few of them.

Question #1--- What is the Flesh and what is the Sprit?

If I am supposed to walk in the Spirit, I need to know what that means, and if I am to avoid the flesh, I need to also know what that means.

My answer came from Galatians chapter five, where Paul tells us plainly what each is.

The Spirit is the Spirit of God, who is known by the fruit of the Spirit, which is actually His character. It is described as; LOVE, JOY, PEACE LONG SUFFERING, GENTLENESS, SELF CONTROL etc.

These characteristics are attributes that define the Spirit of God. There are nine listed, but the Bible referrers to them all as one, singular, not plural.

Question #2---How do I walk in the Spirit?

Is there a magic formula? Can I memorize a script? As I dug deeper into the scriptures, I found my answer…To walk in this Spirit is to let the fruit of God's Spirit manifest, grow and live in you.

This is what becoming more like Christ or Christ-like means. When we walk in love, we are walking in God's Spirit. When we demonstrate self-control, we are walking in God's Spirit.

When we are filled with peace, even though confusion is all around us, we are walking in God's Spirit. That goes for joy and all the rest of the attributes.

We display the fruit of His Spirit in our lives and thereby show forth His glory upon the earth.

Some might argue: *But what about me?* They would say, "To allow Godly attributes to flow from my brings, when I am really a short-tempered and selfish, denies me the right to exist and sets up a phony two-faced persona that will ultimately drive me crazy, because I can never really attain that elusive Christ-like nature. I want to be ME, whatever that is, and it will take me a lifetime of exploration and emotional self-expression to find it."

Paul struggled with this "I want to be me" scenario more than anyone and wrote to the Roman Christians in his letter saying,

> *"And be not conformed to this world: but be ye transformed by the renewing of your mind, that ye may prove what is that good, and acceptable, and perfect, will of God."* Romans 12:2

From the beginning, God designed us to be filled with and walk in His Spirit...why? So He could have fellowship with us.

Think about that. He wanted to communicate with beings of His own creation, that were on His level...not gods, but children of God. This is higher than the angels, able to create, think, reason, plan, wish, dream and be the likeness of God in the earth.

We all know that Adam was the prototype of such a being, and he rebelled against God, seeking to live outside of His love in a self-awareness that denied God the pleasure of his company. Man's will was aimed at self-realization based upon his own reasoning and power.

All that God wanted for him was lost because he no longer dwelt in the Spirit of God. Even his love became distorted, and his whole reasoning fell into a selfish gratification.

God's race of godly children, fashioned in His own likeness, was lost, seemingly forever. Man became a distortion of mind and body that led to a worldwide flood, a sentence of death for all who are called human after Adam's kind.

We also know that it was God who designed a plan of redemption and set it in motion, even before the foundation of the world.

That plan was Christ crucified, once for all, that whosoever believes in Him, this Jesus of Nazareth, who died as a penalty for sin, who was made sin for us, might have eternal life.

He came to seek and to save that which was lost…the Love, Joy, and all the other attributes of His personality. Man can once again fill the earth with God's image and likeness.

We only need to watch the evening news or read the morning newspaper to realize the depravity, rebellion, and self-realization of man.

It is all vested in pornography, fornication, same-sex marriages, murder, road rage, divorce, hatred, and a host of other deeds that emanate from what Paul calls, the Flesh or natural personality of man. He is referred to as the "Old Man" that is void of God's Spirit.

We are left with a choice: walk down the road of fleshly appetites or up the road of God's destined path for His children. It is truly a matter of free will.

We ultimately decide our own future. The choices we make today shape our tomorrows.

We can be transformed from wickedness into righteousness, from lust and immorality into love and respect, from confusion and sorrow to peace and joy, from death unto life by the renewing of our minds. I, or the, "ME," with the heart that Jeremiah says is desperately wicked, must die before the new life of Christ can flourish.

I finally figured it out. It is like a grain of wheat. If it is not planted, it abides alone and the newness or life in it cannot be expressed. But if it falls to the ground and dies, or is planted, it will bring forth new life. This is the principle of resurrection.

The old passes away, and out of its death comes a completely new creation. The choice to give up our life is to understand that God will replace it with a new one that is fashioned after Him.

We get rid of the desperately wicked heart and grow a new one that is full of love, joy, peace and all the goodness of God. It is most commonly referred to as being "Born Again."

We are reinstated into His original destiny. He never wanted man to experience evil, but he did…so now we are left to choose between good and evil, deciding which will express itself in and through our personality.

Question #3 – How do I get from the flesh to the spirit?

We must deny the expressions of the flesh. That means, when we feel sad, we give thanks to God and rejoice in the knowledge of His love.

When we are caught up in confusion, we ask the Lord for peace and so on. However, the move from one to the other is not always a hop, skip and a jump. Often, it is the hardest thing we will ever do. Why, because one must die in order for the other to live. That is why Jesus told His disciples that they must take up their cross and follow Him.

The cross was, and figuratively still is, an instrument of death. It is where life is extinguished through great suffering. We will suffer with Him if we deny anger access to our emotions, for it is in the emotions that anger, and all the other ungodly traits, raise their nasty heads. They will fight us for life and expression.

Let them live, and they will distort and destroy all that is good. Nail them to the cross, and they will die.

The Bible says that the Spirit and the flesh war against each other and are contrary, the one to the other. They both strive to be seen, heard and showcased in human flesh. Galatians 5:17.

The flesh, which is no more than fallen man without God, full of pride, jealousy, lust, anger, adultery and so forth, has no need for God.

The spirit, on the other hand, seeks after the things of God and enjoys the status of His likeness. Our souls are caught in the middle, in the valley of decision with eternity hanging in the balance.

Paul shared his struggle as he passed through this valley of decision. He cried out, *"who shall deliver me from this body of sin? Then he said, Thanks be to God."*

If you cannot seem to get out of the flesh to walk in the Spirit, cry out to God and ask Him for a personal rapture where He calls you up out of the miry clay and sets your feet on solid ground. His hand is not too short that it cannot reach down and save you.

His ear is not too dull that He cannot hear your cry for help. It takes only a repentant heart and a serious desire to follow Jesus, even unto death…that is, the death of the flesh.

When you cry out, do not be surprised if God uses other people to nail you to the cross. He often uses that which is most aggravating to get your attention and keep it.

A final thought…Paul says in his letter to the Philippians, the third chapter,

> *"Finally my brethren, rejoice in the Lord" "Beware of dogs, beware of evil doers" "for we are the circumcision which worship God in the spirit and rejoice in the Christ, Jesus and have no confidence in the FLESH."* Philippians 3:2

We are to live and move and have our being in Him, (The Lord).

Walking in the Spirit of the living God depends directly on having no confidence in the flesh. This means that I can no longer count on my emotions, feelings, instincts, and other human traits to guide me unless they line up with God' will. Now, I used the knowledge of God's Word and applied it to each situation.

Like Paul, I declared that what things were gained to me, those I count as loss for Christ.

> *"I count all things as loss to gain the Excellency of Christ."* Verse 7-8

I realized I must let go of the petty issues and attitudes of this life to gain true fellowship with my Heavenly Father, through Jesus Christ, His Son. Verse 10 of Chapter three says it all.

> *"That I may know Him and the power of His resurrection, and the fellowship of His suffering, being made conformable to His death."*

We will never know Him until we conform to His death on our own cross. In other words, putting the fleshly appetites to death so that the Godly attributes may live and shape our future.

What I further realized is that each time I walk in the attributes or fruit of God's Holy Spirit, I am having fellowship with Jesus. I can actually walk in His shoes and think His thoughts. I can feel His heart beating in me.

I say all of this because I know myself, and I am normally not like Jesus. I am filled with jealousy, bitterness, pride, selfishness, and many more negative traits.

I guess you need to know yourself before you can see Jesus in you. For me, It is a miracle to see the hand of God in my life.

CHAPTER THIRTEEN

The Great Epiphany

Have you ever come to a realization that changed your life? I have had several. The greatest revelation was when I discovered that God really loved me. No fooling, He really loves me and He really loves you.

I struggled to believe that at first because I seemed to always be doing things that broke His commandments... things like well; we won't go into all of that now. I am sure you know what I mean.

I was raised with a low self-esteem. My eyesight was not the greatest because of a brain hemorrhage when I was a baby. I am guessing when I say that, not totally sure. I did not do well at school.

My learning ability was slower than other kids. The school suggested that my parents take me to a clinic where they can test my brain waves to see if I was retarded. Fortunately for me, I passed the test and was declared normal.

That meant I was just lazy. In actuality, I had an eyesight problem. Once I was moved to the front of the class and wore glasses, I did better.

How do I know that God loves me? What is it about me that He loves? Why does He love me? All these questions and more kept flooding my mind until one day I read John 3:16. It said,

> *"For God so loved the world, that he gave his only begotten Son, that whosoever believes in him should not perish, but have everlasting life."*

God's love is not equal to our feelings. If we feel unloved, God still loves us. Our feelings are not a measurement of His love. He is always with us. His love is unconditional. It does not depend on what we do or not do.

"I AM" THERE

"I AM" There,
At the end of your broken dreams,
Before the sun rises over your day,
Prior to those tear-filled streams.

"I AM" There,
Down that road of despair,
When all seems to be lost,
And no one seems to care.

"I AM" There,
Over all of life's twists and turns,
When tomorrow is all but gone,
And when you are full of concerns.

"I AM" There,
Sayeth the Lord of Host,
To bring you hope and peace,
And the power of my Holy Ghost.

"I AM" There,
To be sure you make it through,

In the midst of every trial,
To bless your life and deliver you.

"I AM" There
Written By John Marinelli

"And, lo, I am with you always, even unto the end of the world. Amen." Matthew 28:20.

God loves us. Every believer knows this, but it is good to hear it again from the scriptures. Here are some of my favorite verses about how God loves us.

> ***Isaiah 41:10*** *– "Fear thou not; for I am with thee: be not dismayed; for I am thy God: I will strengthen thee; yea, I will help thee; yea, I will uphold thee with the right hand of my righteousness."*

> **Romans 8:31** *-- "What shall we then say to these things? If God be for us, who can be against us?"*

> **1 John 4:18** *-- "There is no fear in love; but perfect love cast out fear: because fear hath torment. He that fears is not made perfect in love."*

> ***I John 4:16*** *-- "And we have known and believed the love that God has for us. God is Love; and he that dwells in love, dwells in God and God in Him."*

As I mentioned above, the God kind of love is unconditional and selfless. It is not brotherly or romantic like we see in this world. This is the kind of love that Jesus introduced to the people of Earth.

It was the God kind of love (selfless) that drove Jesus to the cross, willingly to be the sacrifice for sin. That is why we worship Him and trust in Him…because He gave all He had for us.

The word expresses the God kind of love in the New Testament, in the Greek language, "Agape." It is the highest form of love that there is. It is also why we can put our trust in Jesus, knowing He is trustworthy.

When I realized how great this love was and still is, I could not help but give my all to Him. It is a miracle that God would even care what happens to me, yet He does care and even rejoices over me. I see His love every day in so many small ways. It is overwhelming.

CHAPTER FOURTEEN

For Love or Money

It all happened when I fell in love with my secretary/office manager. That was 43 years ago. She was and still is a beauty.

After a few months, the Lord visited me. He rang my doorbell and asked for a drink of water. I told him to come on in and charged him $125 for the bottle of water.

If you believe that, I have a bridge for sale that will fit all your travel needs.

Here is what really happened. I was recently divorced, living in South Florida. I was an executive managing a Chamber of Commerce.

It was a new job for me. I came in like a whirlwind with new programs, fundraising ideas, and committees. I also implemented policies I learned when I was the director of Big Brothers & Sisters in central Florida.

Long story short…three secretaries quit on me because I overworked them. They were used to having coffee and chatting all day about nothing. That left only one secretary, who was new on the job.

So, I promoted her to office manager and married her six months later. When I interviewed her for the position, I found her to be well-qualified, shapely, and otherwise WOW!

We hired other staff and went on with the business of being a Chamber of Commerce.

In the meantime, I rededicated my life and talents to Jesus. I was an ordained Southern Baptist minister who had lost his way.

My newfound love was also a Christian of about one year. She was full of questions and brave enough to ask them during working hours.

I would try to answer them, but because I was still recovering from being spiritually shipwrecked, I relied on my historical knowledge of the Bible instead of offering a simple spiritual application.

I guess I frustrated her a lot back then. She could easily see right through me. She knew I was not where I should be spiritually. I had no joy, no peace and certainly no walk with God. It was all superficial. She would regularly ask me, *"Why are you mad at God?"* She wanted to know what had happened to me.

One day I took the time to tell her. I had been married before. It lasted for 10-years and I had custody of two small children from that marriage.

I had been through mental mind-games and sexual manipulation. However, I had prayed that God would fix what was wrong so I could still raise my kids. I was a good father and loved them.

God did not fix anything yet. He did fix everything, just not in the way I expected. For a short while, I was mad at God because I was about to lose my kids.

I remember one specific time when praying that I heard the voice of God saying, *"Can you forgive me?"* Now I knew God does not lie and can do nothing wrong. He needs no forgiveness from anyone, certainly not from me. However, I broke into tears and said, "Yes, Lord."

Then I began to see why it had to be the way it ended up. I just was not meant to be with her. She became an alcoholic, remarried and divorced again, and died a few years later.

She resisted me at every turn, from answering the call to be a minister, how I disciplined the children, and a lot more.

I finally felt free and alive again after my divorce but empty inside from all the trauma of a failed marriage. That is until I hired this New York lady, who later became my wife.

Just so you know, she was never married before marrying me, and I did have scriptural grounds for divorce.

Shortly after we married, I again heard the voice of the Lord talking to me in my spirit. He said,

> *"you can't have your new wife and the job at the Chamber."*

I immediacy knew what he meant and why he was saying what He said.

My new wife was a new Christian with a strong desire to follow Jesus. She was pulling me to her so we could have a life together under the authority of the Lord.

On the other hand, I was the Chamber Boy. It was highly political, charged with deception and full of liberal thinkers.

Do not get me wrong. I enjoyed my job and was the "fair-haired" boy, liked by most everyone. That is as long as I kept my faith to myself, laughed at their off-color jokes, and fell in line with their expectations.

God had put me in the valley of decision. It was a choice between love and money.

The job brought a good salary, lots of single women and publicity from the local press. However, my spirit was longing to serve the Lord like I had before, and my heart was smitten with my love for my new wife.

It was a hard decision for me to make. It took about 30-seconds. I resigned my position and held on for dear life. It was going to be one hell of a ride.

I found myself unemployed in a poor economy. It was seven months before I found a good-paying job. However, it was all worth it. God worked everything together for good, and we are still serving the Lord together.

It is a miracle that we made it this far, but we did. God seems to be in the business of making miracles happen.

Over the years we formed The Fellowship of Christian Poets and ran it for over 10-years. We registered almost one million visitors and hosted the largest Christian poetry library in the world.

We also formed and still operate Have A Heart For Companion Animals, Inc., a not-for-profit animal concern agency with a website visitation rate that is over 166,,000.

CHAPTER FIFTEEN

Ketoacidosis Coma

Diabetic ketoacidosis is a serious condition that can lead to a diabetic coma (passing out for a long time) or even death.

When your cells do not get the glucose they need for energy, your body burns fat for energy, which produces ketones.

Ketones are chemicals that the body creates when it breaks down fat to use for energy. The body does this when it does not have enough insulin to use glucose, which is the body's normal source of energy.

When ketones build up in the blood, they make it more acidic. They are a warning sign that your diabetes is out of control or that you are getting sick.

My lovely wife did not know she was diabetic. We were not looking for the signs. She was just exhausted and slept most of the time.

I knew there was something wrong, but she would not go to a doctor. She was not all there to make rational decisions. After a few days and a worsening condition, I forced her to go. I took her straight to the emergency room of a nearby hospital.

By the time we arrived at the emergency room, she was delirious, coming in and out of reality. The attending doctors said that she had "diabetic ketoacidosis," which led to a coma.

The doctor then told me I had better prepare myself for the death of my wife. He said that she would either pull through and live or slip into a coma and most likely pass away. It could go either way.

The worst part was that now that she was in the hospital, I could not be with her because of the COVID-19 virus restrictions.

So I went home and prayed. I gave thanks to God for my wife and prayed for her complete recovery. I said to God, "It's okay if you want her to go home to you, but I'd like to have her here with me as long as I can."

Then I started a telephone calling buzz and an email blitz, letting everyone I could think of know her condition, prognosis, and outcome.

They all said they would pray. Many posted my call to prayer on their Facebook page and other social media platforms. One friend told me later that there were over 1,000 folks praying for her healing.

She was in the hospital ICU for six days and then went to a rehabilitation facility for another nine days before coming home. She then spent 2-3 weeks in-home care with nurses, occupation therapy, and physical therapy.

Most of the hospital stay was in and out of a coma. She does not remember much, just bits and pieces here and there. She had post-traumatic amnesia.

Once home, she began using insulin and took a bunch more pills that regulated her high blood pressure and potassium levels. **(B12 and Staton drugs)**

The good news is that she lived and did not die. She was on 25 units of insulin twice a day. With a strict diet, she slowly came down to not needing insulin anymore. She was judged to be prediabetic with an A1C level of 6.2. It was a miracle.

The miracle got even better when she received her health records. The records showed:

- Kidney Failure
- Diabetic Coma
- Pneumonia
- Confusion
- Low Potassium
- High Blood Pressure
- High Cholesterol
- Low B-12

She ended up with a 40-lb weight loss and is in good health today. It is a miracle that she pulled through.

CHAPTER SIXTEEN

The Covid-19 Attack

My wife came home in May, and I went into the hospital in mid-September.

It all started with a fever that lingered on for four days and then came shortness of breath. I kept putting it off, thinking I could handle it. But it was too much. I was getting worse.

I ended up at an urgent care facility breathing oxygen. I had a full-blown case of COVID-19. There were no vaccines at that time. They transferred me to the main hospital by ambulance, where I stayed in the ICU for 18 days. I was in the hospital for 23 days.

They hooked me up to continuous oxygen, gave me pills and shots every day and watched over me for signs of getting better or worse.

I was so bad that I had to wear a heavy breathing mask at night that forced oxygen into my lungs to keep them from collapsing.

I had both bacterial and viral pneumonia. My lungs were

on the verge of shutting down. This was besides the COVID-19 virus.

One doctor told me that if I did not start getting better soon, he would have to put me on a ventilator. Most people never get off that machine. They just die.

One of the folks attending to my needs said that he was proud of me for fighting so hard. He went on to tell me that most people die when they were as bad as I was.

My wife was heading to the hospital to see me when she saw the Lord in a vision. He was standing over me with the devil lurking in the background. She was driving when all of this happened, yet she did not crash.

The Lord said to her, "This is my battle." Then He leaned over me with His body stretched out, touching mine. I did not see or feel anything, but I started feeling better.

I came home a week later to home healthcare until I could function normally again.

I have some side effects from the virus, like hair loss and vocal box obstructions that keep me from speaking clearly. However, they told me that this too will soon go away.

I experienced the love of God and the touch of Jesus firsthand. It is a miracle that I am even alive.

CHAPTER SEVENTEEN

The Anointing

Do you believe in miracles? I do. I have seen them happening firsthand. I was filled with the Holy Spirit in the first year that I was saved. It was a "By Faith" experience.

Unlike so many that came before me that spoke in tongues or were slain in the Spirit, I felt nothing and had no tingling experience.

I was a Southern Baptist, and they were deep into Bible knowledge but mostly rejected the gifts of the Spirit, saying that they stopped when the last apostle died.

Their rationale did not make sense to me because it was the gifts of the Spirit that validated Jesus' ministry and the Apostles' authority. The gifts set the early Christians apart as "Little Jesus" folk.

It was hard for me to accept that the gifting of believers was no longer needed. After all, the earth's population grew from around 300 million to 7-8 billion. It would only make sense that the gifts would be needed more in this generation than any other.

So, when I was a young Christian, the Holy Spirit anointed

me to minister and preach the good news that God loves us and Jesus died for us so we could be saved.

I have seen the anointing knock people down that were standing; heal broken bones; deliver folks from diseases or tormenting devils; soften hard-hearted souls; bring joy and laughter to otherwise sad hearts; and bring fresh revelation to a confused mind.

I ended up with the better of the two theological perspectives. Though they were diametrically opposed to each other and a source of bitter controversy, they blended perfectly in my Spirit.

It has been over 70 years, and I still enjoy the fresh revelations from the Holy Spirit. I marvel at the way God blesses and delivers His children through the operation of spiritual gifts.

It has been a ride of a lifetime. I have soared like an eagle to new heights in the Spirit. I have walked in the Spirit with Jesus and had fellowship with the Father. I have prayed for and laid hands on suffering saints and watched as the anointing took over and healed them.

The Bible says…

> "But if the Spirit of him that raised up Jesus from the dead dwell in you, he that raised up Christ from the dead shall also quicken your mortal bodies by his Spirit that dwells in you." Romans 8:11.

I am now in my latter years but still alive to God and open to the anointing power of His Holy Spirit.

HOLY SPIRIT

Holy Spirit, Lord divine
Send your love and make it mine.
Come, Lord Jesus, for all to see.
Holy Spirit, breathe on me.

Holy Spirit, Lord divine
Fill my heart with new wine.
Come, Lord Jesus, hear my plea.
Holy Spirit, breathe on me.

Holy Spirit, Lord divine
Be my Lord, all the time.
Come, Lord Jesus, is my plea.
Holy Spirit, breathe on me.

Lord of glory, I come to Thee.
Holy Spirit, breathe on me.

Written By
John Marinelli

CONCLUSION

Life is an adventure. If it is not an adventure for you, it could be. You must see with your spiritual eyes.

Some folks that I brushed shoulders with over the years shared with me they were living a nightmare. They had no vision; no hope; no reason to even exist. In their own words, they said, *"We were just taking up space."* How sad that a person would feel that way.

I have strolled down memory lane and called attention to those adventures where I could see the hand of God. I call it, *"A God In Action Adventure."* I am glad you came along. I hope you were inspired and blessed.

Let me challenge you to take a stroll down memory lane. However, do not look at the sadness or sorrow. Instead, focus your thoughts, rehearsing the good stuff, where you saw God in action. You may discover that the Lord has been there all along, helping you to make it through.

It has been great to go back and see the Lord at work on my behalf. It has strengthened my faith and my resolve to walk with the Lord in this world. I will stay the course and fight the good fight of faith and always give thanks to God for His love and grace.

ABOUT THE AUTHOR

John Marinelli

Rev. Marinelli is an ordained minister. He formed and was pastor of one church in Wisconsin and was the pastor of another in Alabama. He has also been a youth minister and evangelism director over the years.

Rev. Marinelli is an author and a poet. He has authored nearly 50 books, most of which are Christian, including:

"Original Story Poems", a children's story poem book", "The Art of Writing Christian Poetry," "Pulpit Poems," "It Came To Pass," "Moonlight & Mistletoe," Mysteries & Miracles," "Believer's Handbook of Battle Strategies,"

"Why Do The Righteous Suffer, "and "How To Live A Victorious Christian Life," and many more.

He is also the author of over 80 eBooks on various Christian subjects. His eBooks are also available on his website.

John is an accomplished Christian poet. He also dabbles in songwriting and writing one-act Christian plays.

He is the vice president of Have A Heart For Companion Animals, Inc., a "no-kill" animal welfare organization.

www.haveaheartusa.org

John is now retired and enjoys life in central Florida. He stands ready to take another faith adventure with the Lord.

www.ingramcontent.com/pod-product-compliance
Lightning Source LLC
Chambersburg PA
CBHW020429010526
44118CB00010B/498